my world within

© Kapil Sibal, 2012

All rights reserved. No part of this publication may be reproduced or transmitted, in any form or by any means, without the prior permission of the publisher.

This edition published in 2012
IndiaInk
An imprint of Roli Books Pvt. Ltd.
M-75, G.K. II Market, New Delhi 110 048
Phone: ++91 (011) 4068 2000
Fax: ++91 (011) 2921 7185
E-mail: Info@rolibooks.com;
Website: rolibooks.com
Also at Bangalore, Chennai, & Mumbai

Cover Design: Bonita Vaz-Shimray
Layout: Sanjeev Mathpal
Production: Shaji Sahadevan
Cover Painting: Pablo Picasso, 1881-1973, München, Pinakothek der Moderne, © Blauel / Gnamm - ARTOTHEK

ISBN: 978-81-86939-63-5

Typeset in Bookman Old Style by Roli Books Pvt. Ltd.
and printed at Rajkamal Electric Press, Haryana.

my world within

Kapil Sibal

Dedication

for

my wife

and

companion

Promilaa

Contents

❧

Part II

Acknowledgements

Meter and rhythm are central to life. The flow of words has a rhythm. There is a rhythmic quality to the wonders of nature. This is why I find it difficult to pen my thoughts in any other way as I seek to discover my 'world within' and 'without'.

Some thoughts in my previous book *"I Witness"* had something to do with my past. This one essentially is about the present.

A lot has happened in the last couple of years. Tumultuous changes have taken place. We have been through a global economic depression. The world was unsure about its future prospects. Nations suddenly realised that the prosperous world is living beyond its means. Yet our integrated economies and unity in action sought to stem the tide of uncertainty. In the midst of all this, we had witnessed terrorist attacks. They shook us. We suddenly realised what a dangerous world we live in. In a sense, we are all unsafe. We don't know when and where terror will strike next to overwhelm us once again. Our politics is in turbulence as the economy waits to surge ahead. We are unsure whether our political system is mature enough to take advantage of the enormous opportunities that await us. Yet beauty lies in confronting the challenges we seek to resolve.

The challenges are even more daunting when we consider the 1.2 billion who are part of our family. Large sections of our people live in both fear and hope. Aspirations are on the rise. The marginalised are learning to hold their head high and ready to be counted. They wish to forget the past, seize the present to create a future for themselves. The burden of the past seems to weigh on their minds. For the minorities, they don't quite understand their predicament. Some of them don't feel at home. Within this complexity lies the beauty of India. Her ability to stand steadfast, attempting to realise our dreams.

Our most important task is to educate our young. A newborn child is pure in every sense; innocent, uncomplicated, safe in the lap of the mother. Negative attributes, including prejudice develop as the child grows to realise the reality of an unjust, unfair and unequal world. Education only helps the child to cope with these harsh realities. Each of us has a 'world within' and a 'world without'. We are aware of the reality within and have to deal with the reality without. Each embarks on a journey to discover the terrestrial and the celestial. Both evoke awe and yet are inherently beautiful.

This is the sense of the journey that I am making. I find beauty in everything ugly. That is the only way I live. Beauty, friendship and most of all love, therefore, are central to life. In some form or the other, love is all pervasive and that emotion is always with us and remains with us. At any given time, that is the most significant emotion. Nature, quality and the subject matter of love may well be different, but that is the only bond that really unites those around us.

Sometimes I wonder whether God fits into all this. Some of our journeys are inherently unjust for no fault of ours. Some of our journeys are ostensibly full of happiness or should be. God's world is in no sense perfect. So how can God be perfect? The only form of matter that I find close to perfection is nature. It needs protection.

This collection of poems is a reflection of what I have said above. My mobile phone has been my close companion in this effort. It is easy to erase all that I don't like. It allows for mobility of thought and place. That makes it a handy instrument for creativity.

The manuscript for this book would not have been possible but for the painstaking efforts of Kundan and Rajesh, who sometimes with their suggestions enhanced the quality of the poems. The ubiquitous Nirmal Singh was always ready to support me in this effort.

I must acknowledge the constant encouragement I got from Priya Kapoor. She often nudged me to complete this effort soon. She has been patient and extremely helpful with her tips.

My wife, of course, is my sounding board and a hint of a grimace helped me correct the rhythm or meter. She allowed me space to rework my thoughts. She also ensured that some of the unprintable poems are not part of this collection. Her true wisdom and unstinted support helped me complete this endeavour.

You inspired me
To etch my thoughts
Pen them down
In broken rhyme

Helped often bare
My heart and soul
For years in
quarantine

Kapil Sibal

PART ONE

WITHIN

Move On

☙

How many battles
can you fight, and
the one within, with
all your might;
how many conquests
will you make, you
just need one
for your own sake.

Rid yourself of
anger and hurt, come
be my mate, I'll
help comfort; with
wounds not healed
your hurt is deep,
I'll kiss you gently
help you weep
wash away demons
from your past,
your future has
a different cast.

The day is clear
the morning crisp,
as you walk ahead
you face no risk.

I know you have
a heart of gold
a lively mind,
a conscience bold,
you always took
the righteous path,
as night recedes, bask
in the aftermath.

Attraction

Lifeless forms
can come alive
with the warmth
that you exude

you scorched me
with, a gentle kiss,
aroused passion
thus far subdued

captivated
felt your embrace
as you held me
with a glance

there was no need
for me to speak
the message was
gently nuanced

the hyphen of
our turbulent lives
dissolved with the
unspoken word

the skyline I
was witness to,
its contours, were
far from blurred.

Enslaved

❧

You enslave me,
bound within the
expanse of your
limitless love,
where I find
freedom.

You absorb me
within your eyes
gifting me with
vision anew,
making me see
myself.

As you bare truth
to the bone, I
float through the
seamless treasures
of your emotive
being.

I find peace as
you help me with
my pace, for I
could lose myself
thinking I was
born free.

Seasonal Desire

☙

As I watch the
outpourings of
monsoon showers,
wait with bated breath
to quench my thirst

you touch me
with your fingertips
as I respond
to the first few raindrops
before the burst
of passion,
when heaven and earth
seek succour, the
one receiving the
other, in trust.

Tender Thoughts

ঌ

Long to caress
the fragility of
your being with
my warm breath
as you awaken
to the softness
of its journey.

Your scarred
soul, needs
gentle flower
petals, to soften
the hurt –
the source of your
deep agony.

Will wean away
the pain, and
cushion you
within the comfort
of our love –
a uniquely composed
symphony.

Distance

The distance of
a thousand miles
makes it difficult
to survive

I long to stretch
my arms to have
all my yearnings
come alive

rejoice in the
flavour of a world
of taste and touch
combined

the texture of
those images are
both earthy
and sublime

you are the
receptacle of love
where comfort lies
unconfined

to be enslaved
by what both
need, our love
not undermined

gives access to
a tranquil state,
of freedom
undefined

would rather have
you far away
than be distanced
from my mind

thoughts in quick
flight, allow me
to, abridge chasms
of time.

Past, Present and Future

☙

Footprints of history
are – yesterdays gone by,
memories linger as milestones
until we say good-bye.

Thoughts are pauses, commas
of a present on the move,
no future lies without a past
with which it is suffused.

Whispers, echo in my mind
your words, the syllables of life
disjointed sentences engulf,
yet make me come alive.

Your touch, a spatial odyssey
on the highway of desire
beckon living dangerously
with every cell on fire.

Our yesterdays gathered pace
making today seem still
it's time for you say to me
will move only if you will.

When the past and present merge
the future lies within,
a future which has no past
has no end, nor beginning

Vibe

☙

The resonance
of words
connects us
to each other

the resonance
of feelings
is what brings
us together.

Swaying with Poplar Trees

I do not know
the reason why
you always end
up, feeling shy.

Is it that you
hesitate, to
tell me how
you feel of late

having explored
have come to know
you always want
a little more.

You will get lost
as we move on
it's like crossing
the Rubicon.

Another world
will come alive
with honeycombs
in our beehive.

The landscape will
be virgin green

gasp at new sights
we haven't seen.

The mind afloat
a gentle breeze
swaying along
with poplar trees.

horizons seem
within our grasp
the past erased
a memory lapse

And when at last
we hit the ground
savour a world
we newly found

then you will know
the reason why
there was no need
to feel so shy.

Lift the 'purdah'
see how time flies
as you touch me
with your open eyes.

The Artist's Soul

ራ

Art forms
may be different
the passion
is the same.

The painter's
and the writer's
soul
is stirred
miles away from
the mundane.

Still Long for You

&

Your absence makes
me miss your smile,
getting used to it
will take a while.

Your childlike ways
sheer zest for life
defied most norms
was not contrite.

This journey was
your very own
though in our midst
yet felt alone.

Searching for stars
amidst galaxies
an unbound ride
through celestial fields.

For years you felt
the winter chill
longed for a sun
static and still.

Dark frozen sheets
a vast expanse

permeate the ice
with a solar dance

the melting surface
warms up and flows
visits new worlds
that no one knows.

It was time for you
to come back home
you knew that I
too felt alone.

Searched my mind
wandered for days
longing for years
in different ways.

You know I missed
you all this while
but most of all
your open smile.

The door for me
is still ajar
convinced that you
are not too far.

Demons of the Past

&

Your scars look fresh
when will they heal?
Your flow of blood
for years congealed.

Why have you let
your spirit wane?
it's time to look
at life again.

Gather your strength
open your eyes
walk away from
those broken ties.

Memories laden,
a painful past,
with prejudices
that are iron cast.

Yesterday's fears
still linger on
destroy all hopes
to be reborn.

Scars when healed
will not efface
those footsteps that
your past have traced.

Present shadows
of years gone by
give tomorrow
another try.

To take a flight
to nowhere land
you just might have
to hold my hand.

And as we walk
on a new track,
embrace life afresh,
do not look back.

Infidelity

☙

An uncut diamond
hard to find
convinced that you
are only mine.

The shiny stones
you talk about,
suggest that you
still have some doubt.

Attracted by
their dubious shine,
I might pick up one
and make it mine.

These shiny stones
are strewn about
do cross my path
while I am out.

Their worth I know
for I can tell
I only wish
you knew me well.

The uncut one
that makes me shine
the only one
that will be mine.

These glittering stones
you know with time
lose out on worth
and also shine.

This uncut priceless
diamond must
celebrate life
and in me trust.

God Unkind

ঌ

When You strike
with lethal force
and slice with ease
through budding lives
to leave a trail
of shattered dreams,
where wastelands of
despair survive

Your artful ways
to paralyse
the lives of those
who need You most,
distraught they seek
deliverance,
each passing day
death is their host.

You haven't moved
mountains for me,
nor witness to
what You can will,
gifted instead
unplanned graveyards,
the world for me
lifeless and still.

Drop manna from
the sky one day,
wretched millions
have looked Your way,
and yet You turn
Your back to them;
Your denizens
have felt betrayed.

The chosen few
who have no faith
are fuelled by
their endless greed;
watch silently
Your generous ways,
for those removed
from want and need.

Lure us to hope
for Paradise
we trust and die
believe it's true
but witness to
this unjust world
would like for once
to question You.

As I await
Your answers, that
might rekindle
my love for You;
my conscience seeks
to question me:
why do I still
pray for You?

Fresh Start

☙

Geared up to start
another year
the past confined
the future here.

The present has
links with the past
our future now
we must recast.

For our own sake
love others who
for their future
rely on you.

Friendship

❧

A special friend
who I can claim
will counsel me
when I complain.

When happy, he
will share my joy
in times of grief
always stand by.

Your friendship is
a gift that's rare
and that is why
I really care.

Mother's Love

☙

I nurtured you
for many months
and when you came
I saw
my love encased
in moulded flesh
beauty naked
and raw.

You battled with
the soft terrain
feeling your way
about

quickly learning
to feed and rest
the world within
your mouth.

You understood
as I did too
the bond that we
had forged

I knew at once
your instant needs

by protests that
you lodged.

The language that
you learnt at first
bereft of words
conveyed

the gentleness
of warmth you felt
the touch of love
that stayed.

You learnt your way
with alacrity
quickly you proved
your might

raring to grab
all that you saw
kept things out of
your sight.

Felt that you owned
all that you claimed

you never learnt
to share

such moments of
eternal bliss
were spent without
a care.

Was time for you
to get to know
the world beyond
your grasp

learning the art
to weather storms,
be punished for
a lapse.

The battles that
you won at first
you were destined
to lose

the time had come
to let you go,

have you decide
and chose.

Stoically I
stood and grieved
aware that you
were hurt

preparing for
what lay ahead
bereft of my
comfort.

Stand upright, face
the world alone,
battling within,
without

you seldom now
take succour from
your mother, when
in doubt.

The time has come
for you to craft
a home, that is
your nest

to partner with
the one who cares,
for you deserve
the best.

In stormy times
when all seems lost
you'll find me by
your side

no matter what
others may think,
for me you are
my pride.

Our bond was based
on love and trust
the way forward
in life

its only when
you shun them both
lose sight of what
is right.

Through love I taught
you how to choose

with trust, the kind
of choice

en route you must
never forget
your conscience is
your voice.

Commerce colours
all forms of love
and shakes the trust
we claim

we value not
their real worth
seek both of them
for gain.

My love for you
your trust in me
no contract could
ensure

without profit
or fear of loss

relationships
endure.

And as you build
your bridges with
the lessons you
absorbed

I hope that you
will follow them
that way you'll get
my nod.

No better way
to march along
give more than you
expect

your days will be
suffused with joy,
not having to fear
what's next.

Parched Terrain

☙

Your lips are parched
the summer dry
each moment seems
like years gone by.

Dried brittle leaves
reduced to dust
oncoming spring
will make robust.

The constant urge,
sprung out of gloom
bless us with an
endless monsoon.

Shower us with
incessant rain
the ground must not
be parched again.

With nectar I
will lace your lips
starting with a
soft, gentle kiss.

Eternal Love

&

There was a time
when you and I
both felt, there was
no reason why,
this love of ours
will wane or die.

When we were young
the urge was high,
we tried to meet
oft on the sly,
seldom gave up
without a try.

As we moved on
and years went by
still longed for you
and I know why:
you really cared
and so did I.

Love's texture had
a subtle dye,
exuding warmth
to testify,
the comfort of
our lullaby.

In combat we
held our heads high,
when elements
were in full cry,
we locked our arms
without a sigh.

The waterfall
was now close by,
above my head
the azure sky
never wanted
to say goodbye.

And as I fell
my throat was dry
our love engraved
in years gone by
lay still, alive
in Cupid's eye.

Worlds Within My World

❧

I reach out to
a world beyond:
see hazy clouds
that wrap the earth,
gaze at the stars
new galaxies
searching for Truth
a quest since birth.

Unique wilderness
that brings to life
silence that is
afloat with ease:
vast sea of space
deathlike and still
a moving morgue
hides mysteries.

Luminous silos
bedecked, they glow
an eerie gloom
yet wondrous sight
reach out to catch
fallen stars, as
we journey through
our spatial flight.

This beginning is
without an end,
there is no change
of seasons here
no monsoon showers
to quench our thirst,
uncharted course
which goes nowhere.

Knowing not how
it all began;
Big Bang array
rich nature's feast
ordained, unplanned
by faith divined
our knowledge yet
far from complete

I want to see
those fireworks
giving birth to
our newborn stars;
where nascent suns
implode within
watching the dance
of cosmic wars.

Nature bursts
within its womb,
it re-creates
to re-align;
tears asunder
her testament
seek solutions
that she must find.

To break away
to bring to life
constant churning
to 're-invent';
yet we embrace
the status quo
central to all
human lament!

My God

❧

I want my God
to smile like me
virile and strong
alive with me.

A comrade who
believes in me
a friend, seldom
agrees with me.

Yet guides me in
my destiny
ensures my mind
is rancor-free.

Our placid gods
are calm, serene
lure us with an
attractive dream.

Those who live by
faith today
their God will pay
them back some day.

Our hopelessness
will keep alive
hope, reason for
us to survive.

This illusion
is *maya's* trap
our short-lived stint
a painful lap.

Mortals beware
the aftermath,
follow the Buddha's
eight-fold path.

Desire, central
to human greed,
embrace a world
sans want and need.

Should I await
a vulture's flight
to find out if
at all you're right?

Or perhaps let
my pyre burn,
ashes afloat
inside an urn.

Saddled around
layers of earth
safely ensconced
within a hearth.

Might be too late
to realise
that your sermons
were not so wise.

Help me now to
find my God
whose counsel I
can learn to applaud.

Need to absorb
the sights I see
find beauty in
what seems ugly.

Your writ should run
for those in need,
a just response
to every deed.

Treasures I wish
to excavate
help my spirits
to levitate

My God of Truth
should partner me
in laughter and
in misery,
this life is what
was meant for me
the other side
is yet to be.

I want my God
be with me now
help me manage
my life somehow.

Reward me before
the aftermath,
guide me along
the righteous path.

If not, my God
is too remote,
conceived to be
an antidote
for those who dare
to be at par
with others who
have travelled far.

Your miseries
have been ordained,
if you lose here
you're bound to gain.

This mirage I
have failed to see,
my God is my
contemporary.

Another Year

☙

Yet another
year went past
like previous years
ever so fast.

I wonder when
you'll lie me down
not here, perhaps
then out of town

finish stories
thus far half told
and start afresh
with those untold.

Will keep our words
frozen in time
you always were
my valentine.

My gift for you
unspoken words,
with feelings laced
that sound absurd.

If not, this year
will pass us by
and next year I
will wonder why

knowing full well
we did not try,
and let another
fresh year go by.

The Silence of Snowflakes

Gentle snowflakes
whisper to me
like wayward minds
have lost their way.

The eerie stillness of
winter nights
bear witness to
their carefree flights.

They sway in silence
and adjust with ease
caress contours
that no one sees

merge as they fall
with comfort lie
their journey is
a lullaby.

I want you by
my side, adrift
you are, for me
sweet nature's gift.

Wayward our ways
an antidote
where distance, time
is kept afloat

this fulsome lap
allows me to
in nature's womb
get close to you.

And as we sink
within our world,
like snowflakes lost
yet closely curled.

Beyond Normality

❧

So far shackled
is what I see
no evidence of
insanity.

It seeks and breeds
a state of mind
where crevices
are for the blind.

Raging bull in
a china shop
none in that state
can make it stop.

Your insanity
somewhat effete,
is manicured
polished and neat.

To be insane
set yourself free
and in that state
belong to me.

Unity

&

Just look around,
within, and see,
the spectacle
of Unity.

Its diversity
often displays
the Oneness of
its many ways.

Truth is oft
hidden, cocooned
embedded in
Sweet Nature's womb.

Matter a speck
in open space
its myriad births
poetic grace.

It never dies
yet changes form
a world bursts forth
all else is calm

the cycle of
mortality
seeks solace in
infinity.

The Truth, Advait
the wholesome He
beyond our grasp
oft scoffs at Me.

That Truth is God
the Force unseen
its attribute
pure and pristine.

Thus spake Gandhi
for God is Truth
the Ultimate
of every route.

Through Ahimsa
be One with All
heeding Nature's
clarion call.

Memories

☙

My skin awaits
your gentle touch
it trickles through
my body's pores
reaches
my all
extremities.
yet constantly
I yearn for more

You occupied
the empty space,
my lingering doubts
were exorcised.

New avenues
had opened up
the past was sought
to be excised.

The present is
the past to be
memory suffused
deep down within

what was before
still part of me
without it I
could not have been.

Raison d'être

☙

I act, therefore
I feel alive
my volition,
helps me survive.

Yet when I act
I need to know
within, why I
have acted so.

I want, and so
I choose to act,
desires' flame
keep me on track.

Intentions are
urged by the self
seeks to preserve
even, in pelf.

Must move beyond
the self to know
why am I here,
where should I go?

The self erased
in nature's plan,
and none of this
conceived by man.

The miracle
of life is lost,
nature consumes
and bears no cost.

The raison d'être
of life, not Me,
but what we are
collectively.

Time

❧

Time never slips
as humans do,
never looks back
like me and you.

It has no form
in constant flow,
what happens next
you never know.

We feel it's might
as we grow old,
fashions stories
so far untold.

It's just, in that,
it pays no heed
no way to stop
for those in need.

Cannot befriend
to help escape,
as we confront
the hand of fate.

The cauldron of
decaying life,
emotionless
it keeps alive.

We race against
it all the time
the 'I' in us
holds on to 'mine'.

The symbol of
infinity
part of cosmic
divinity.

Consumes with its
relentless force,
time moves ahead
without remorse.

A Friend Who Passed Away

❧

When last I rang
the phone was cut
tried reaching you
but just could not.

I never knew
that you had gone,
never let out
why things went wrong.

Called up to hear
the voice I knew,
to find out how
things were with you.

The ring was proof
you were around,
found solace in
a simple sound.

Its absence raised
some doubts at first,
hoped for the best
yet feared the worst.

You were alone
with none to care,
relentless fate
had not been fair.

Your mother came
with the three of you,
married again
with hope renewed.

Earned laurels in
your years at school,
proved to your mates
you were no fool

at Rutgers earned
your law degree,
yet life never
was hassle free.

You had your sights
on partnership,
they turned you down
you lost your grip.

New York seeks out
new worlds that blend,
where strangers pose
as long lost friends.

Unbound unleashed
full lives undone,
where vultures swoop
down as you run.

Lost stories as
the traffic rolls,
Testoni shoes
old socks with holes.

The good condemned
to dead-end streets,
where demons toast
unjust defeats.

In cruel climes
a child of peace,
could not combat
conspiracies.

You reached out to
a father who,
for years chose not
to think of you.

Discomfiture
was in the air
rejected, felt
unloved uncared

Let yourself go,
lost out on pride
gave up the fight
to turn the tide.

Your triumphs now
were gourmet meals,
German success
at soccer fields.

Road to nowhere
your very own
would end up, not
answering the phone.

Summing Up

❧

Young budding star
a sheer delight,
embarking on
a virgin flight.

Where syllables
are strung in words
while older folk
behave like nerds.

Seeks life beyond
his comfort zone
explores the world
but not alone.

Senses he is
in full command,
satisfaction
upon demand.

Tests waters for
approving nods,
triumphant as
we all applaud.

The 'Ya Ya' house
where nani lives
in paradise
for she forgives.

With 'dadi ma'
sticks on like glue,
convinced that she
is only two.
Knows 'dadi ma's'
and 'nani's' are
the greatest of
them all by far

When favoured with
a wet slobbering kiss,
cruise through the day
in utter bliss.

Each moment's like
a treasure chest,
cannot resist
his constant quest.

Learns as he falls
walks as he learns,

by now he knows
can't set the terms.

Of what is left,
thus far unknown
those conquests will
be on his own.

Will have to think
before he walks
not babble on
before he talks.

Make judgements based
on what he learnt,
no instant balm
when fingers burnt.

Now is the time
to hug and kiss,
Kodak moments
that we cherish.

Alight Aboard

ॐ

I saw, I felt
that this was it,
soon, have you love
me, bit by bit.

Took me sometime
to make you think,
of feelings, that
take years to sink.

The road ahead
was blocked at first,
the task was to
develop trust.

I understood
the way you felt,
how in the past
the cards were dealt.

The comfort was
that I felt sure
that you in time
will feel secure.

Now that we know
how we both feel
prepare ourselves
for a new deal.

Know of pitfalls
that are ahead,
we understand
what's left unsaid.

Together hold
each other tight
to step aboard
a heady flight.

Partnership

☙

You helped me wade
through thick and thin
advised me oft
where to begin.

Prised open doors,
lost treasures shown,
you never made
me feel alone.

When sprinting, you
softened my pace
taught me how, then,
to run with grace.

You nursed my wounds
when I was hurt
absorbed the pain
gave me comfort.

Without your love
tough to survive
your presence makes
me come alive.

Change

❧

Standing structures
will fall apart
creased with age
rusted with fatigue.

Static, unmoved
condemned with time
resisting change
that we all need.

Moving waters
cleanse as they flow
through pastures that
they had not seen.

Carve out a course
through fresh terrain
conquer new worlds
and dare to dream.

'Thooku Ramani'

❧

The emptiness
we felt for long
we waited for
you all along.

'Thooku Ramani'
a dream come true
for us you are
a special brew.

Angelic looks
belie what lies
beneath, eager
mischievous eyes

tip the nipple
refuse your feed,
oblige us when
you are in need.

For now it is
a one-way street
you, Captain Cook;
we are your fleet.

Your orders we
must understand
through gestures, signs
of your own brand.

You grieve and we
must wonder why,
you smile, that has
us heave a sigh.

Our world is tense
you are at ease
choosing to do
just as you please.

We are villains
unfair, unjust
and yet we are
the ones you trust.

Your milestones are
our highs, that we
will store them, etched
in memory.

Lost Treasure

ঌ

You continue
to caress my
thirsty, parched mind,
give it succour;
as memories
of the past, are
washed ashore, like
silent waves in
the dead of night,
reaching out, yet
ebbing into
ocean waters;
submerged with
the senseless din
of mundane moments.

Within, I miss
the turbulence
of love that swept
us off our feet
as its embers
scorched our skin
festering wounds
that hurt, yet kept
alive the love;

you turned away
I knew at once
what came to pass.

All I could do
then, was whisper,
holding your hand.

The Past Embedded

ঌ

The present I
own, not the past;
then why should I
its burden share?

The womb that gave
me birth and more,
my past perhaps
embedded there.

Genetic traits
evolved with time
the building blocks
of living cells.

No reason to
reject, that which
unknown, belongs
to me as well.

Today I am
is what you see,
the past within
me, races through.

The essence of
my very being
of which I have
no real clue

erased with time
yet I will live
along with those
who follow me.

A hyphen that
I am, will know
sustain all those
who come to be.

Wifely Muse

☙

Sweetheart do keep
your evening free,
last time I called
your secretary,
was curtly informed
that it would take
sometime before
you took a break.

At other times
wait patiently,
you're off to your
constituency;
when you return
past dinner time
in that melee
lost track of time.

I understand
that busy men
seldom get home
till after ten,
by then I feel
nothing is right
losing out on
my appetite.

Watch you, hungry
swallow your food
now you are home
I must not brood;
why don't you set
some time apart
forget the past
make a fresh start?

When last you did
get dressed to go
to watch with me
the latest show?
I saw a crowd
stand by the gate
yet once again
they sealed my fate.

Their tales of woe
melted your heart
our trip ended
before the start.

I always wait
stand in the queue,

I want to be
in front of you.
Hope for a chance
to lead the way
so that I too
might have a say.

What I have said
perhaps not new,
and yet I can't
stop loving you.

PART TWO

WITHOUT

Our Seedlings

&

The sculptor's eye
the painter's brush
the symphonies
that music brings

make lifeless forms
come alive
pulling gently
at our heartstrings.

Teachers have space
and years to sculpt
to mould, to carve
to paint with ease

with nature's gift
fine-tune the mind
help make them drive
their destinities.

Give vision to
blind-folded minds
contour new paths
for curious eyes

have them respond
to others' pain
essential for
all human ties.

You nurture them
with loving care
ignite them with
what helps sustain;

these seedlings are
our future trees
bring showers to
our parched terrains.

Food for Thought

☙

The duality of women
a few can understand,
males perceived as symbols of
a uni-dimensional brand.

Ordained by fate to multitask
do three things at a time,
preserving human species
is nature's grand design.

Our symbols of temptation, the
power behind the throne
when empowered, gallop at
a steady pace alone.

With attributes of grit and steel
sensitive to concerns,
unafraid of challenges
for 'good' seek no returns.

The millions un-empowered now
gathering the will to fight,
hoping to see them take off
on a heady flight.

This is not Cricket

࿐

One day a beloved leader
had a disturbing dream,
was called upon to play for
the Indian cricket team.

Knowing that he could not bat
his bowling underhand,
why selectors took a chance
he could not understand.

All his attributes he felt
unsuited to the game,
that was indeed the reason
none objected to his name.

Did not believe in fair-play
and if the game looked lost,
was prone to tamper with the ball,
must win at any cost.

Infiltrate the opposite camp
to work behind the scenes,
reach out for their key players
adopt unsavoury means.

Expressed his no confidence,
appealed on every ball,
did all he could to influence
the third umpire's call.

Such leaders are of a rare breed,
we value not their worth,
must look out for technologies
to help us sight them at birth.

The Fissile Left

❧

The Left has suffered
for a lifetime now
from an ailment
they can't diagnose;
the symptom, however,
that troubles them most
is that they
cannot just see
beyond their nose.

Doc Basu warned them
of the precipice ahead,
gave them medicine
to prevent them fall,
the healer Surjeet
with practical tips,
weaned them away
from the *Das Kapital.*

They were then advised
to see an optician
for a possible
vision transplant,
for alternative
ways to prosperity,
for the poor who
suffer from want.

Manmohan with
solution in mind,
said he would do
whatever he can,
had to listen to him
beyond the regime
of, the 'common
minimum programme'.

To see beyond the nose
we must energise
the mind, clogged
confused and unfree;
Doc Manmohan believed
as studies revealed,
the only way out
was the '1 2 3'.

Convincing those
with vision impaired,
facing their ire
and opprobrium
was no mean task,
for what he needed
was, a steady
supply of uranium.

This fissile material
with reactors in
place, would aid in
clearing the mind,
but fossilized thoughts
ranted and raved
saw opposition,
complete and blind.

Frustrated he thought
that in changing track

he had an outside
chance to succeed,
without energy supply
his patients would die,
the afflicted needed
time to concede.

With objectives achieved
their minds will mutate
helping them to
re-learn, as they see,
his actions he thought
might just clear the way
to rework their
ideology.

Walking without Crutches

❧

Give me the tools
to wake me up
with freedom that
might help me smile.
For centuries,
my strength was sapped,
felt lost, useless
wasted, sterile.

I want to learn
the alphabet
string words to help
me slowly climb,
that ladder of
opportunities
you duly scaled
while in your prime.

These crutches that
you chained me with
to save me from
being stranded,
I cannot dare
unchain myself,
feel exposed
marked and branded.

The only way
to shed my skin
and fight the taint
that's born with me,
is to make me
believe that I
can fashion, my
own destiny.

I want no favours
no alms as help,
signals to show
that I am weak,
treat me as one
who at birth learns
to walk pathways
all others seek.

I have the rights,
to learn like you
I'll show you who
I want to be,
without crutches
I wish to ride
the only way
I can be free.

John, the Muslim

❧

Delivered without a name
Allah was not known to me,
of Ram I was yet to learn
the Lord Christ I could not see.

Ma I had lost her at birth
Hindu Pa I never saw,
parents adopted me
oblivious of who I was.

I looked like other children
my blood group did not reveal
the religion I was born to
I had nothing to conceal.

Parents were of Muslim faith
had chosen to name me John,
belief in human brotherhood
thought that I was Christian born.

Everyday they offered *namaz*
I learnt at last to offer too,
the true meaning of Allah
was not difficult to construe.

Christ did forgive the errant
this was taught to me at school,
Allah, Christ were both benign
known to be the Godly rule.

I learnt from my Hindu friends
the meaning of righteous ways,
the centrality of tolerance
their scriptures amply displayed.

Why must I be a Christian?
Or embrace my parents' faith?
my ancestors were Hindu
this I got to know of late.

The blood cells in my body
and the oxygen I breathe,
all my body's functions are
not part of any creed.

My close friend Asim at school
I know he cannot claim, that
he breathes any other way
though he has a different name.

Name, source of identities
not of our beliefs and faith,
and when we confuse the two
become harbingers of hate.

Religions seek to deliver us
to a world that is unknown,
all sins committed thus far
He is likely to condone.

Religion provides recourse to
escape from all sins en route,
He who forgives wrongdoers
is open to rebuke.

All faiths that breed violence
their own God will not forgive,
if He does, we might question
the raison d'être to live.

The Mullahs, Pundits and the Priests
all those preaching brotherhood,
seek to protect and cherish
values for human good.

I am John the Muslim, a
Christian, Hindu, all in one
believer of faiths that love,
and yet am slave to none.

All faiths must subsume within
love for every human being,
history of man sadly belied
the hope, that could have been.

I Matter

Was held static for centuries
now want to own my skin
sprint alongside others
to find my strength within.

Cascade like water molecules
which sparkle as they flow
keen to discover new terrains
to set my mind aglow.

Inherited an inglorious past
with the sun forever set
carried with me its burden
life's journey under threat.

Debarred thus far to see the sky
gaze downward and transfixed,
even my surreptitious dreams
were meant to be eclipsed.

Was told that I was born in chains
marked by nature to servility,
and if I chose to breach my fate
would be target of hostility.

Tortured and mentally lynched
at the bottom of the rung,

my ancestors were rudderless
silenced and unsung.

Made to walk apart, without
an anchor to guide or mould
resigned, as all would pass me by,
stayed put, did as I was told.

Took centuries for me to stand up
while others walked in days,
mumbled for years before I spoke
was treated as a prey.

I dare to walk, have learnt to speak
now weigh what I am worth,
find that millions march along
witnessing my rebirth.

As I mingle with the crowds
am empowered to be free,
time for them to realise
that I too have a destiny.

Rat Race

☙

Was I born to loose
this race that I was
born to run,
or is it that no one
will win, no matter
how well we run?

Only a Name

&

Why is Ashraf
my enemy?
That happens to
be my name.
My parents, my
co-conspirators,
they too must
share the blame.

Six letters of
the alphabet,
a burden I
carry for life,
they look at me
suspiciously
quietly I
swallow my pride.

They strip me of
all my virtues,
seeking a peek
into my mind,
in search of dark
demonic traits,
associate them
with just our kind.

Randomly get
taken to, where
they believe I
truly belong,
a prisoner of
my identity,
am convicted
without any wrong.

Targeted as
the enemy, know
not with whom
I am at war,
to find out who
the demon is,
they don't have to
venture too far.

The enemy
resides within
their hearts, full of
deep prejudice,
afraid to face
the reality,
cognizant of
what is amiss.

My name is just
a lame excuse,
to wage a war
they have to fight,
in doing this they
entrap themselves
blur the contours
of wrong and right.

My name is now
a seedling that,
grows to suspect
and learns to hate,
would loath to be
who you think I
am, act before
it is too late.

Prejudice

&

Give me the space
where I can breathe,
secure, that I
am truly free,

don't look at me
suspiciously
questioning my
very right to be.

I was born with
a predictable name
and that too was
given to me,

don't look for answers
I do not have
which you seem to
want from me.

Who will answer
the questions, I
often ask, quite
persistently

you think I might
be one of them
the moment you
set eyes on me:

my name, attire,
the way I look,
seem proof of my
culpability.

Such questions you
must ask yourself
keeping your mind
from bias free,

if not, you have
no right to ask
all those questions
so insistently.

You make me feel
unwanted in
what for years has
been home to me,

my forefathers
and all their dreams
are buried here
since centuries.

Don't tear asunder
my very being
destroying all that
is dear to me,

don't take away
what I cherish most,
that is an intrinsic
part of me.

My ancestors too
had shed their blood
sacrificed their
future for me,

there is no parting
of ways, together
we share, an uncharted
common destiny.

In our quest, I was
always a part
of you, and you
a part of me,

within the expanse
of your open mind
don't carve out some
territories for me.

Assign me not
a separate space
where you think, I
ought to be,

and if you try
to cast me thus
it means that you
too, are not free.

If you truly are,
don't be a slave
to prejudices
about me,

the demons that
we are looking for
reside within both
you and me.

Let's find the demons
within ourselves
then alone we will
break free,

after which you
will see yourself,
whenever you
look at me.

Walk the Talk

&

To make your dreams
come true
that is my dream
for you

it's time to talk
with you
seek ways to walk
with you.

Will Rise to Quell the Storm

&

We understand
our nation's grief,
watch silently
in disbelief

yet wonder why
this had to be,
your targets are
faceless, and me

eager to hear
when you will fall
the fervent prayers
of one and all.

We'll triumph when
you're limp and still
knowing that you
were paid to kill.

He gave you life
rare precious gift
your violent end
gruesome and swift

your Allah too
will not pretend
your charred remains
a welcome end.

Victims knew not
that you would write
their last chapters
before the night

not give them time
to say good bye
take stock of life
before they die.

For them we'll rise
to quell the storm
our innate strength
will be reborn

their lives will not
be lost in vain
nor will ours be
the same again

Necessary Evil

&

Our polity
cannot survive
they seek us out
to help them thrive.

Notorious,
known by our deeds
we understand
their unique needs.

We criminals
are a disgrace
we occupy
a special place.

They recognize
our innate worth
the rationale
for our rebirth.

The elected seek
priority
we too deserve
security.

Commandos flank
protect each side
our chest swells up
with righteous pride.

Feel overwhelmed,
our country cares,
to combat threats
that are not there.

Responding to
our real needs
protect us from
our own misdeeds.

Stall cases, have
charges withdrawn,
empower us
to move right on.

Cover us with
a secure net
payback time
for unpaid debts.

Black sheep with the
help of Black Cats,
democracy
might just collapse.

This killer virus
is breeding fast
our politics
must be recast.

Change the actors
revamp the stage,
turn over to
another page.

Retaliate

&

I feel entrapped
just like you do.
You by your acts
and I by you.

You target me
yet you are blind,
product of an
imprisoned mind.

Your freedom comes
with your last breath
for me, when I
escape from death.

No questions asked
when you will die
those mourning me
will question why.

Evil triumphs
snuffs out the flame
our answers are
always the same.

Have fortitude
need to be strong

we'll find out why
and what went wrong.

Engrossed in these
macabre thoughts
saw him fire
two lethal shots.

My neighbour slumped
limp by my side
I sank within
nowhere to hide.

Closed my eyes tight
prayed silently
the next one might
be meant for me.

Each moment
held my destiny
amidst this dance
of savagery.

'Get up and move,
stand by the wall',
shaken by his
rough rasping call,

lifeless shuffles
with slothful moves
we dragged ourselves
with bloodstained shoes.

Lined ourselves up
against the wall
wanted to make
just one last call

to tell you that
all roads are blocked
I'll miss you till
my heartbeat stops

tell the kids that
I won't be there
to help them walk
ahead with care.

I never knew
at death I'll face
bullets, and not
a warm embrace.

Daring to look
I saw him smirk

knew that he soon
would go berserk.

They laughed as if
this was a game
and mockingly
gave it a name:

'Nine Pins'
ready to fall,
their weapons aimed
to make the call.

From one side his
comrade would shoot,
the other end
would follow suit.

I heard the sound
of gunshots when
I fell, before the
count of ten

thought I was dead
yet was surprised
lay still, buried
opened my eyes.

The sound of boots
peels of delight,
their trophy was
this deathly sight.

As I passed out
felt someone kick,
faintly remember
a camera's click.

Felt Satan's trap
in vile embrace
confronted death
right in the face,

wondered if I
was still alive
no reason for
me to survive.

He leaves this choice
to those who kill
comfort ourselves
as being God's will.

This terror strike
was not His call
why then should those
beside me fall?

Remember wise
Krishna's discourse
your duty now
is to use force.

Fruitless now to
negotiate
take aim to kill,
don't vacillate.

Will not buy peace
at any cost
cherished freedoms
must not be lost.

The End of Tolerance

&

Vibrant Mumbai
stared, pulverized
a safe haven
was jeopardized

ten demons tried to
deplete its soul
felt hopelessly
out of control.

Café Leopold
caught unawares
terrorists planned
to strike in pairs.

Elegant dome
preserved its pride,
Taj suffered, was
not mortified.

Trident ablaze
by terror's web,
days crimson red
long nightfalls bled.

Fractured the peace
of Moshe's house

aimed to destroy
without a grouse.

Commuters at
the CST,
unmindful of
their last journey.

Our monuments
of collective grief
will mourn all souls
not meant to leave,

their porous walls
absorbed the pain
frozen relics
of acts insane.

Rare fortitude
courageous acts,
spirit felt bruised
yet kept intact.

And as we stitch
our broken lives
remember lost
husbands and wives,

our daughters, sons
and soldiers brave,
all those we tried
but could not save.

Fresh tender wounds
take years to heal
their flow of blood
static, congealed.

Mumbaikars are

a different breed
to unjust threats
never concede,

stand phalanx-like
in combat mode
fiercely protect
their home, abode.

Will spare no one
not any more
will kill, before
you come ashore.

The Art of Denial

☙

Ajmal Kasab
trained to be
a terrorist,
Pakistani

want us to prove
what they have known
a terrorist
one of their own

his parents at
Faridkot claim
this is our child
the one they named

since then they have
been whisked away
where they are now?
no one can say

be upfront, says
Nawaz Sharif
your version
is beyond belief

denial of
open access,
why bar parents
to meet the press?

house out of bounds,
most Indians feel
you'd rather have
the truth concealed

your plea, government
unfairly blamed,
Ajmal a known
familiar name

spin doctors too
will not agree
of a grand Indian
conspiracy

Ajmal belongs
to 'no man's' land
challenge us if
at all you can

birth registers
do not contain
a baby blessed
with Ajmal's name

non-state actors
you deftly back
their whereabouts
cannot be tracked

arrest, wanted
Azhar Masood
will vitiate
our national mood

arresting him
would not be right
we have no means
to extradite

the fallback is
we are in doubt
do not quite know
his whereabouts

we did admit
erroneously
that he is in
our custody

if you question
our honesty
will deny his
identity

pastmasters we
have played this game
cannot hang us
just by a name

how many times
will you deny
the world now knows
the reason why

protect Kasab
and meet your fate
in time you will
disintegrate

Global Meltdown

☙

The meltdown of 2009
its genesis
mortgage, sub-prime;
the financial world
felt at a loss
global leaders
met at Davos,
the mood effete
somber with gloom
steps needed to
avert a doom,
global markets
in recession
much like the 30s
Great Depression.

This laissez-faire
has come apart
the end is here
rebuild and start,
late Adam Smith
cannot provide
a recipe
to turn the tide,
the Keynesian way

might help revive
our ailing banks
their erstwhile pride,
toxic assets
to be excised
from balance sheets
and kept aside.

Capitalize
the banks, to see
beginnings of
a lending spree,
restore the trust
consumers need
with new money
let assets breed,
help another
spiral to start
that too in years
will come apart,
the greenback helps
consuming ways
will hearken back
the good old days.

Borrow before
you earn, and spend
consumption is
the only end,
indebted you
might be, so what,
still you are a
most happy lot,
deficits reflect
growing demand
the market is
the magic wand
that has collapsed
values have bust
and bankers too
have lost all trust.

The world has changed
since Brettons Wood
finance is meant
for global good,
our Wall Street czars
must tread with care
for Main Street is
the real player,

regulation
provides the key
coupled with real
transparency,
investment banks
attempt to lure
their profit motive
distilled and pure.

Financial structures
when put in place
need to display
a human face,
rich must prosper
so must the poor
our thoughts alone
will not ensure,
new global banks
must help sustain
those afflicted by
financial strain,
prevent collapse
and devastation
financial systems'
aberration.

The corporate world
must take the lead
seek wealth without
avarice and greed,
dupe not holders
of equity
the key word is
integrity
values, ethics
must underscore
the desire to
acquire more
revamp, reform
inspire trust
make sure the system
is robust.

The Bazaar of Politics

ꟹ

This electoral feat
our grand bazaar
shows us up for
what we are.

It is indeed
a numbers' game
with wooing of
coquettish dames,

some suitors are
easy to net
while others make
you frown and fret.

Fat dowries are
clearly in vogue
known charlatans
not seen as rogues.

Infidelity
is commonplace
all players have
fallen from grace.

Separations and
a quick divorce
in current times
without remorse,

new paramours
will show the way
waste no time in
idle foreplay.

Vital statistics
will keep on track
all those who wish
to share the shack,

multiple partners
in the bridal suite
the ultimate
ceremonial feat.

Empower Me

☙

I do believe
that I must Be,
charter my own
lost destiny

feel free within
imprisoned walls,
my spirit soars
my body crawls

corrupted, used
deprived, enslaved,
committed thus,
am to the grave

sans access to
the world around
condemned, confined
chained to the ground

and yet I seek
to turn the tide
to swim across
the other side

besieged, I drown
yet yearn to float,
in hopelessness
I cast my vote

empower me
in your domain
equations won't
then be the same

Allow me to run

☙

Please rid me of
this awful load
preparing for
the class ten board.

My thirsty mind
craves to create
not have exams
decide my fate.

My curious mind
yearns to explore
much beyond my
classroom doors.

My dreams should not
be cut to size
because I hate
to memorize.

If you test me
for brains and guile
don't have to look
at percentiles.

Marks encourage
one-upmanship
a free ride on
an ego trip.

With textbooks I
should start to surf
inquiringly
look for new turf.

Walk away from
the trodden path
and not invite
my teachers' wrath.

Solving a sum
will not help find
real answers for
a questioning mind.

Create the space
for me to run
let learning be
a lot of fun.

Marauders

❧

Marauders of
this cosmic force
they plunder on
without remorse;

our bounteous earth
provides a feast
we treat it as
industrial yeast.

Disgorge treasures
consumed by greed
trampled by crude
human stampedes.

Through mindless acts
crush nature's womb
these resonate
impending doom.

Human vultures
will starve for want
a deathly morgue
will be our haunt.

The future lost
with our forays
unless we mend
our present ways.

Riding Dangerously

(Recipe for the opportunist)

☙

Politics an
unruly horse,
cantors and trots
all in due course.

Reigning in the horse
takes time and more,
for years you stand
outside the door.

If you wait for
your turn to come
well thought out plans
will be undone.

You push, you shove
shuffle up front
poised and ready
for those who hunt.

Sing paeans for
the thoroughbreds
get closer to
those up ahead.

Sometimes you ride
and pull a horse
let down a friend
for another source.

Alliances
are seldom kept
so long your needs
are left unmet.

Must learn how to
anticipate
jockey and trip
a running mate,

deprive him of
a racing berth
to get a sense
of his real worth.

In the stable
must always try
to catch hold of
the leader's eye.

Blind faith and trust
are virtues which
will help you soon
to strike it rich.

If under siege
do not stand by
rise to defend
don't question why.

The leadership
will look to see
and calibrate
your loyalty,

and if you fail
to be steadfast
the chances are
you will not last.

Having chosen
a bumpy ride
do not despair
if cast aside.

Final Lap To Nowhere

☙

Conflict between
dharma, adharma
underscores our
daily travails

we seldom pause
to reason why
adharma often,
than not, prevails.

Encouraged by
Me, for the I,
never fails to
win the day

envy, intrigue
ambition, lust
provide mortals
our feet of clay.

Some cry out in
the wilderness
give up kingdoms
for a horse,

others gamble
kingdoms away
never waiver
from dharma's course.

Krishna's guile
Arjuna's skill:
triumph in war
justice at stake

yet at what price
and for what end,
were trophies won
for virtue's sake?

We all forsake
our kingdoms for
kama and *artha*
are dharma here

and seek, at last,
solace in Him
our final lap
leads to nowhere.

Frustration

ꙮ

The charred remains
of years gone by
seek answers, though
my wounds are dry.

Etched memories
ugly yet fresh
clothed with concerns
that none address.

Then why should I
lie still and calm?
Those victimized
had done no harm.

Their barren look
saw life abate
that choreographed
violence, undraped

the cult of hate
bred on itself
protectors too
were loath to help.

The frenzy of
the crowds exhumed
decaying, putrid
minds, consumed

to break the peace
not let us sleep,
dark silence that
is ours to keep.

The venom of
the haunted mind
blurs reason when
justice is blind

spews poison when
you least expect
for violent ways
violence begets.

Justice is all
that's left to seek
those left behind
are far from meek.

If you fail us
we have no choice
but to convince you
that we have a voice.

The language which
we speak will show
how we will match
you blow for blow.

Missing Out

ಹ

Those who bore, stay
conventional
most often, one
dimensional.

Look not beyond
their nose to see,
life in its full
diversity.

A wife, a home
a comfort zone,
a garden where
roses are grown.

A bank account
fattens with time
Testoni shoes
that always shine.

All meals on time
health foods consume,
landscape must not
be out of tune.

Quiet evening walks
with dogs on leash

shelf, classic works
like *War and Peace.*

At home nothing
is out of place
the objets d'art
add to the grace.

Crackers and cheese
with fruity wine
summer cruise down
the river Rhine.

Nine holes at golf
weekend routine
cut business deals
on pastures green.

For those who have
lived life this way
unmindful of
the Judgement Day,

you'll know that you
prospered and thrived,
but missed out on
being alive.

Unscripted Path

&

Don't burden me
with scripted words
feed answers, am
obliged to know.

Inspire feed
my quest for search,
whet appetite
longing for more.

Let me inhale
the oxygen
help me surmount
concerns and fears.

Spirit within
seeks to escape
from paths traversed
in bygone years.

My chiselled mind
will breach all walls
to float across
clear cloudless skies,

afresh to view
the universe
reflect again
on how and why,

the playing fields
I want, will change,
discourses we
for years sustained.

Shortsighted goals
with visions blurred,
free spirit was
enslaved and tamed.

Let virgin thoughts
burst forth and bloom
in artful ways
unknown thus far.

Vast galaxies
a fertile space
will help produce
our global stars.

Neighbourhood

❧

My neighbour says
'you're stuck with me;
will harass you
relentlessly.'

It's hard to change
the way he thinks
what with special
external links,

that prop him up with
hardware and more,
diverts their use
to settle scores.

'Will bleed you with
a thousand cuts',
we must concede
no ifs and buts.

Will infiltrate
disturb your peace,
kill innocents
with casual ease.

Often tried to
negotiate

hit a brick-wall
culture of hate.

And yet I need
to compromise
must tolerate
his blatant lies;

infiltrators
stoutly deny
the backing of
the I.S.I.

Disclosures made
clearly suggest
most terror acts
at their behest,

shuns logic and
the proof at hand
the Taliban
a global brand.

Our message is
polite and firm
the proof we have
you must not spurn.

Give samples of
the voice of those,
regarded by
some as heroes.

Collaborate
with outcomes show
our confidence
in you will grow.

Neighbours seldom

cooperate,
the lessons of
history till date.

Committed to
diplomacy,
cannot alter
geography.

With power let
our neighbour know
cannot alter
the status quo,

move away from
your strident stance

pay heed to what
our people want,

they pray for peace
and tranquility
embrace norms of
civility.

Terrorists must
be exorcized,
their venom to
be effectively neutralized.

Dismantle their
structures within
that recipe
will make us win.

It's time for this
mayhem to cease,
the road ahead
must lead
to a lasting peace.

A New Voyage

☙

The limits of
my mind, set free,
help me to think
creatively.

Let boundaries of
learning dissolve,
solutions will
slowly evolve.

Don't chastise me
for failures which,
my efforts then
will help enrich.

Will falter as
I seek to learn,
this process will
help me discern,

my voyage of
discovery
where I will find,
the real me.

Help me perform
my very best
align it to
our national quest.

'Gandhi'

&

Epicentre of a quake
moving to strike
at the roots of
Empire.

A sea of
humanity
surged as
the Pied Piper
mesmerized them
with his simplicity
and sheer grit.

He armed himself
with resolve
conviction and a
God-like sense
of justice.

He strode like
a colossus
his yardstick
Dharma, with which
he measured
his own actions
to empower

the self and
show the way.

Yet, he
who won
us our freedom
was victim to
the onslaught of
un-free minds.